Animal Partners

7/15
ALL OUR LOVE!
SANTA & SABBA

by Scotti Cohn
illustrated by Shennen Bersani

Disastrous Dinner Party

The birds arrived by threes and fours,
promised an eating spree.
The plates and cups were all in place;
the food was fresh and free.

The hostess, in her feathered gown,
was pouring the plankton tea,
when all at once the dining table
sank beneath the sea!

Croc Dentist

Behold the wily crocodile.
Who will scrub his pointy smile?
Who will hop between those jaws,
defying all of nature's laws?

Some folks say a plover's beak
cleans those choppers cheek to cheek.
Others say it isn't so.
I wonder if we'll ever know?

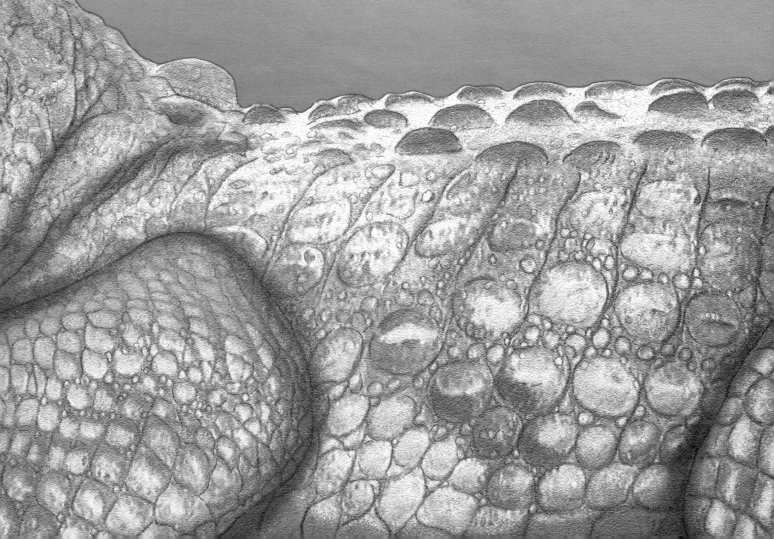

Sea Turtle's Lament

Barnacle, o barnacle,
where'd you come from, barnacle?
Were you born or were you hatched?
How'd we come to be attached?

We're not alike, as you can see.
Why are you so stuck on me?
And why my foolish fascination
with such a clingy, crude crustacean?

Killer Coat

The forest mouse is a stylish bloke;
he wears a beetle cap and cloak.
Fleas find out against their will
this sassy rodent's dressed to kill.

Once at home, his outerwear
scurries all around his lair,
dining on the bugs that stress him
until it's time again to dress him.

Pom Pom Prizefighter

Put up your dukes (or fins or flukes).
Watch me bob and weave.
Go ahead and make my day!
I'd hate for you to leave.

My precious sea anemones
deliver a nasty sting.
I have no fear of enemies
so step inside the ring!

The Mongoose Spa

Free at the Mongoose Spa today:
a yogurt herbal tea buffet,
a mango pear tahini scrub,
a fig and aloe body rub.

Warthog snorts, "Is this for real?
Banana facial? Power Peel?"
He shakes his bristly head and sighs,
"Please just pick the ticks off, guys!"

The Emperor's Clothes

All hail the royal emperor shrimp!
His style is known from coast to coast.
His purple gloves and orange robe
change color just to match his host.

This trick is meant to hide him well
from carnivores who aren't so nice,
including predators like me,
who cook him in a pot with rice.

False Scorpion

Who's that freaky little guy
clinging to the bottle fly?
I know his name, but I forgot
it only tells us what he's not.

We hardly know that he's among us;
we'd never notice if he stung us.
We rarely see him riding by,
clinging to that bottle fly.

Little Mack Attack

Looking for lunch, my fine-finned foe?
Perhaps a mackerel snack "to go"?
It's true that you're a larger fish,
but you will never get your wish.

You think that you're the big kahuna,
but you are just a bluefin tuna.
You'll have to hunt me where I dwell:
here at the Man-of-War Hotel.

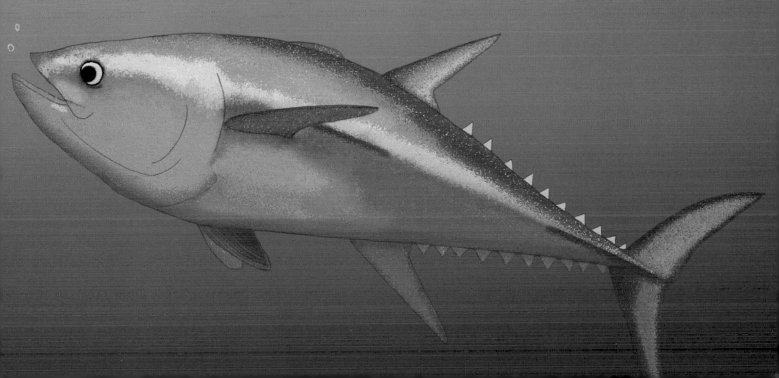

Tickbird's Free Lunch

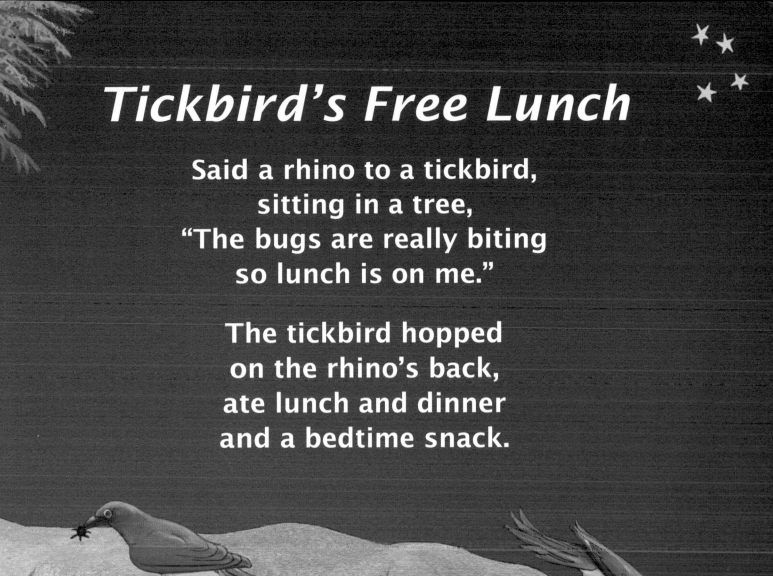

Said a rhino to a tickbird,
sitting in a tree,
"The bugs are really biting
so lunch is on me."

The tickbird hopped
on the rhino's back,
ate lunch and dinner
and a bedtime snack.

That's Remora!

When Remora is bored
and feeling ignored,
she needs to get away.

She loves to embark
on the eight o'clock shark,
headed for Coco Cay.

Full Service Fish

Save yourself some aggravation!
Come on by The Cleaning Station!
To get a special weekly pass,
see our owner, Mr. Wrasse.

Barracuda, eel, or ray,
we will send you on your way—
shiny, sparkly, squeaky clean—
ready for the silver screen!

Casa Iguana

Little Sally Lightfoot,
stands on her tiptoes,
reaches for a treat
with her dainty claw.

Soaking up the sunshine
at Casa Iguana,
she dines on tick sticks
and algae slaw.

For Creative Minds

Helping Partners

Living in the wild can be hard. Not all animals can survive by themselves. Many animals live in families or even larger groups (herds, flocks, pods, etc.). Some animals team up in a close partnership with other kinds of animals. These pairings are called symbiotic relationships. There are three types of these relationships:

- A "**win-win**" relationship (**mutualism**) means that the animals help each other and depend on each other to meet their own needs.

- In a "**win-stay the same**" relationship (**commensalism**), one animal benefits but the other one is not hurt or helped.

- One animal in a "**win-lose**" relationship (**parasitism**) wins by hurting the other animal. For example, a flea on a dog is a parasite. These insects guzzle blood to live. To get the blood, they attach themselves to dogs or other animals. The host dog or animals does not benefit at all. The parasites can pass germs that cause diseases.

What Type of Partners?

Mutualism: One partner eats bugs and parasites from the other animal partner. The one partner gets food and the other partner stays clean.
- When whales come to the surface for air, red phalaropes (a type of sea bird) eat parasites from their backs.
- Egyptian plovers are sometimes called "crocodile birds" based on observations that these plovers pluck bits of meat from the teeth of open-mouthed crocodiles. Scientists are still studying this relationship.
- Up to thirteen beetles cling to the Costa Rican cloud-forest mouse's fur and face, eating fleas. When the mouse sleeps, the beetles eat bugs in the mouse's burrow.
- Banded mongooses eat ticks from warthogs.
- Tickbirds eat ticks and flies from the backs of rhinoceroses.
- Sally lightfoot crabs eat algae from marine iguanas that live on the Galapagos Islands.
- At a "cleaning station," wrasses eat parasites and algae from fish and eels. They might even swim into the mouth and gills of the fish being cleaned!

Mutualism: One partner uses the other one to scare away predators or to attract prey. The smaller partner eats food left over from the larger partner's meal.
- The boxer crab holds a sea anemone in its pincers, waving it to scare away predators.
- Atlantic horse mackerel live between the tentacles of the Portuguese man-of-war. Somehow they avoid being stung and are protected from predators. The fish's bright colors, as well as its small size, attract prey for the man-of-war.

Commensalism: One partner rides on the other partner without hurting the ride-giver.
- "Fake scorpions" (pseudoscorpions) catch a lift from flies and other insects by holding onto legs or abdomens.
- Remoras cling to sharks and a few barnacles hitch rides on sea turtles or whales.

Commensalism: One partner hides from predators without hurting their animal partner.
- Emperor shrimp avoid predators by hiding on the skin of sea cucumbers.

Parasitism: Some good relationships can turn bad.
- A few barnacles hitching a ride on a sea turtle may not hurt the sea turtle (commensalism) but too many barnacles may cause the sea turtle to not be able to swim as well, hurting the turtle.
- If tickbirds peck at and draw blood from backs of rhinoceroses, they end up hurting their "friends," turning a mutualistic relationship into a parasitic relationship.

Match the Animal Partners

Find the animals partners that belong together.

barnacle

Sally lightfoot crab

mackerel

red phalarope

fake scorpion

Portuguese man-of-war

whale

sea turtle

fly

marine iguana

beetle

tickbird

mongoose

wrasse

emperor shrimp

eel

sea cucumber

rhinoceros

Costa Rican cloud-forest mouse

warthog

Match the Habitat

Which animal partners live in the ocean and which live on land?

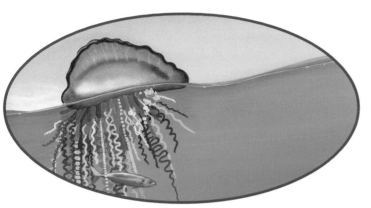

mackerel/Portuguese man-of-war

beetle/Costa Rican cloud-forest mouse

mongoose/warthog

emperor shrimp/sea cucumber

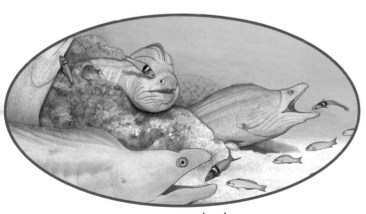

wrasse/eel

tickbird/rhinoceros

Answers: Ocean: mackerel/Portuguese man-of-war; emperor shrimp/sea cucumber; wrasse/eel; Land: beetle/Costa Rican cloud-forest mouse (rainforest); banded mongoose/warthog (African savanna); tickbird/rhinoceros (African savanna)

To my family, with whom I share a mutualistic ("win-win") relationship.—SC
While doing research for the illustrations, I cruised out to Stellwagen Bank Marine Sanctuary on a New England Aquarium Whale Watch boat. Out on the sea I, in awe, witnessed humpbacks and minke whales breaching and feeding. My heartfelt thanks goes out to my family and friends for their continued support of my work. *Danke vielmals*—SB
Thanks to Science Writer Loran Wlodarski for verifying the accuracy of the information in this book.

Library of Congress Cataloging-in-Publication Data

Cohn, Scotti, 1950- author.
 Animal partners / by Scotti Cohn ; illustrated by Shennen Bersani.
    pages cm
 Audience: Ages 4-9.
 Audience: K to grade 3.
 ISBN 978-1-62855-448-9 (English hardcover) -- ISBN 978-1-62855-456-4 (English pbk.) -- ISBN 978-1-62855-472-4 (English downloadable ebook) -- ISBN 978-1-62855-488-5 (English interactive dual-language ebook) -- ISBN 978-1-62855-464-9 (Spanish pbk.) -- ISBN 978-1-62855-480-9 (Spanish downloadable ebook) -- ISBN 978-1-62855-496-0 (Spanish interactive dual-language ebook)
 1. Symbiosis--Juvenile literature. 2. Animals--Miscellanea--Juvenile literature. I. Bersani, Shennen, illustrator. II. Title.
 QH548.C64 2014
 577.8'5--dc23
                                2014009718

Translated into Spanish: Parejas de los animales   Lexile® Level: 750
key phrases for educators: animal groups, symbiotic relationships
Bibliography:
"All About Barnacles." ©2003-2004 *Journey North Teacher's Manual*. Annenberg Foundation. Accessed 3/20/14. learner.org/jnorth/tm/Barnacle. html.
Ashe, James S., and Robert M. Timm. "Probable mutualistic association between staphylinid beetles (Amblyopinus) and their rodent hosts." 1987, *Journal of Tropical Ecology* 3:177-181, Cambridge University Press. Accessed 3/20/14. https://kuscholarworks.ku.edu/dspace/bitstream/1808/5563/1/Ashe&Timm1987.pdf?origin=publication_detail.
Bester, Cathleen. "Sharksucker." *Ichthyology at the Florida Museum of Natural History*. Accessed 3/20/14. flmnh.ufl.edu/fish/Gallery/Descript/LiveSharksucker/LiveSharksucker.html.
Britton, Adam. "Crocodile myths #1 - the curious trochilus." September 6, 2009. *Croc Blog*. Accessed 3/20/14. http://crocodilian. blogspot.com/2009/09/crocodile-myths-1-curious-trochilus.htm.
Calkins, Mandy. "Cleaning Crew on the Reef." August 1, 2010. *Science and the Sea*, ©2006-2012 The University of Texas Marine Science Institute. Accessed 3/20/14. scienceandthesea.org/index.php?option=com_content&task=view&id=307&Itemid=6.
"Cleaner Wrasse." *Marine Animal Encyclopedia*. 2012 Oceana. Accessed 3/20/14. http://oceana. org/en/explore/marine-wildlife/cleaner-wrasse.
Clipperton, John. "Emperor Shrimp – Periclimenes imperator." September 16, 2011. Marine Habitat magazine. Accessed 3/20/14. marinehabitat.co.uk/species-profile-periclimenes-imperator-emperor-shrimp/.
Duermit, Liz. "Caretta caretta: Loggerhead." 2007. *Animal Diversity Web*. University of Michigan Museum of Zoology. Accessed March 20, 2014. http://animaldiversity.ummz.umich.edu/accounts/Caretta_caretta/.
Harvey, M. S. "Pseudoscorpions of the World, version 2. 0." 2011, *Western Australian Museum*, Perth. Accessed 3/20/14. museum.wa.gov.au/catalogues/pseudoscorpions.
Hooper, Celia. "Fur-Cleaning Beetle Jumps From One Exclusive Designation to Another. " September 18, 1988, *Los Angeles Times*, United Press International. Accessed 3/20/14. http://articles.latimes.com/1988-09-18/local/me-3253_1_large-beetles.
"Indo-Pacific Periclimenes Shrimp (An Overview)." October 13th, 2008. *Morphologic Blog*. Accessed 3/20/14. http://coralmorphologic.com/b/2008/10/13/indo-pacific-periclimenes-shrimp-an-overview.
Leao, Mark. "Remora remora." *Animal Diversity Web*. University of Michigan Museum of Zoology. Accessed 3/20/14. http://animaldiversity.ummz.umich.edu/accounts/Remora_remora/.
Lougher, Tristan. "Boxer Crab." 2007. Courtesy of *Marine World Magazine*. Accessed 3/20/14. aquariaworld. co. uk/invertebrates/boxer_crab. htm.
Mark McGinley, Sylvio G. Codella, Patricia Gowaty. "Mutualism." Encyclopedia of Earth. November 19, 2012. National Council for Science and the Environment. Accessed 3/20/14. eoearth.org/article/Mutualism?topic=58074.
Miller, Nick. "Grapsus grapsus / Sally Lightfoot crab." *Animal Diversity Web*. University of Michigan Museum of Zoology. Accessed 3/20/14. http://animaldiversity.ummz.umich.edu/accounts/Grapsus_grapsus/.
"Red Phalarope." *Bird Web*. Seattle Audubon Society. Accessed 3/20/14. http://birdweb.org/birdweb/bird/red_phalarope#.
"Rhinoceros." *African Wildlife Foundation*. Accessed 3/20/14. awf.org/wildlife-conservation/rhinoceros.
Rumelt, Reid B. "Phalaropus fulicarius." June-July 2012. Brief natural history summary of Phalaropus fulicarius. *Smithsonian's National Museum of Natural History*, Washington, D. C. Accessed 3/20/14. http://eol.org/pages/1064981/overview.
"Symbionts, Parasites, Hosts, and Cooperation-MarineBio. org." *MarineBio Conservation Society*. Accessed 3/20/14. http://marinebio.org/oceans/symbionts-parasites.asp.
"Symbiosis: Mutually Beneficial Symbiotic Relationships." ©2002, *President and Fellows of Harvard College*. Accessed 3/20/14. causalpatterns.org/resources/ecosystems/pdfs/s5_res_symbiosis.pdf.
"Warthog Meet Mongoose." *National Geographic* Education video. ©1996–2014 National Geographic Society. Accessed 3/20/14. http://education.nationalgeographiccom/education/media/warthog-meet-mongoose/?ar_a=1.

Manufactured in China, November 2014
This product conforms to CPSIA 2008
First Printing

Arbordale Publishing
Mt. Pleasant, SC 29464
www.ArbordalePublishing.com